# Suzuki®

## CELLO SCHOOL

Volume 4
Piano Accompaniment
*Revised Edition*

GW00645210

© 2003, 1983 Dr. Shinichi Suzuki.
Sole publisher for the entire world except Japan:
Summy-Birchard, Inc.
Exclusive print rights administered by
Alfred Publishing Co., Inc.
All rights reserved.   Printed in USA.

ISBN 0-7390-5366-3

# INTRODUCTION

*FOR THE STUDENT:* This volume is part of the worldwide Suzuki Method of teaching. The companion recording should be used along with this publication. A cello part book is also available for this material.

*FOR THE TEACHER:* In order to be an effective Suzuki teacher, ongoing education is encouraged. Each regional Suzuki association provides teacher development for its membership via conferences, institutes, short-term and long-term programs. In order to remain current, you are encouraged to become a member of your regional Suzuki association, and, if not already included, the International Suzuki Association.

*FOR THE PARENT:* Credentials are essential for any Suzuki teacher you choose. We recommend you ask your teacher for his or her credentials, especially those related to training in the Suzuki Method. The Suzuki Method experience should foster a positive relationship among the teacher, parent and child. Choosing the right teacher is of utmost importance.

In order to obtain more information about the Suzuki Association in your region, please contact:

International Suzuki Association
www.internationalsuzuki.org

# CONTENTS

(The **Minuets** from the Suite in G Major by J. S. Bach in the Cello Part book are unaccompanied.)

# Sonata in C Major

## Op. 40, No. 1

Jean Baptiste Bréval
(1753-1823)

**Allegro**

10

Rondo grazioso

# Adagio and Allegro
from the Sonata in E minor, Op. 1, No. 2

Benedetto Marcello
(1686-1739)

**Allegro**

# Chanson Triste

Op. 40 No. 2

Piotr Illyich Tchaikovsky
(1840-1893)

**Allegro non troppo**